A BLACK PARENT'S HANDBOOK
TO EDUCATING YOUR CHILDREN
(Outside of the Classroom)

BARUTI K. KAFELE

Baruti Publishing
Jersey City, New Jersey

For information regarding quantity discounts or any other inquiries and questions about the book, please write or call:

Baruti Publishing
P.O. Box 4088
Jersey City, NJ 07304
Attn: Baruti K. Kafele
(201) 433-9484

Cover Conception, Illustration & Design: Evan Dawes

Typesetting: Kimberley Broughton-Kafele

Photography: Edward V. Walker, Jr.
Family picture by Haneef Akbar

Second Printing

Library of Congress Catalog Card Number: 91-91992

ISBN: 0-9629369-0-1

DEDICATION

"A Black Parent's Handbook" is dedicated to all Black parents, for the responsibility of educating "our" children rests on our shoulders.

If we fail in our responsibility, we will have committed a "grave" crime, indeed.

ACKNOWLEDGEMENTS

This is a special thank you to five wonderful African women who continue to provide me with strength, support, confidence, motivation and faith in their own big ways. They are: my mother, Ms. Delores Jenkins, my wife, Mrs. Kimberley Broughton-Kafele, my grandmother, Mrs. Roselle Smith (Nana), my aunt, Mrs. LaVerne Jenkins-Dawes and my mother-in-law, Mrs. Lillie M. Broughton.

I would also like to thank four influential African men in my life: my father, Mr. Norman G. Hopkins, my father-in-law, Mr. Samuel Broughton, my uncle, Mr. Walter T. Dawes and my good friend, Mr. George E. Cushnie.

Thank you to my "models" in the pictures who made this book complete. They are: Doshon F. Drake, Aja Broughton, Samuel S. Broughton, Mr. Samuel J. Broughton, David Cushnie-Bell, Ms. Gail Cushnie-Bell and Ms. Delores Jenkins.

Lastly, a super thank you to my wife, Kimberley, for her tireless work in typesetting, arranging and editing this book. You're a life saver!

ABOUT THE AUTHOR

Baruti is a Brother who has immersed himself into his Blackness. He is a student of African history and culture and sees these and education as the key ingredients to our liberation.

Brother Baruti was born in Orange, New Jersey and participated in athletics throughout elementary and high school.

He earned his Bachelor of Science degree in Management Science/Marketing and educated himself in African/African-American history. He is currently working on a Masters degree in Elementary Education and has educated himself in this field as well. Brother Baruti was destined to teach, whereas his mother and father have over fifty years of teaching experience between them.

As a student at Kean College of NJ, Brother Baruti was inducted into Who's Who in American Universities and Colleges, 1986 (as Norman A. Hopkins, his former name), Phi Kappa Phi National Honor Society, Lamda Alpha Sigma Liberal Arts and Sciences Honor Society, graduated Summa Cum Laude and received the Black Student Union Academic Achievement Award as the number one ranked Black male student in the college.

Brother Baruti had a brief stint in politics as an elected member of the County Committee in East Orange, NJ. He has tutored and taught children on the elementary level for four years and has lectured on a variety of topics throughout New Jersey. Most importantly, he desires to always remain a strong role model for Black youth.

Lastly, Brother Baruti is a committed family man. He is married to a lovely wife, Kimberley and is a proud father of a beautiful baby boy, little Baruti, whom he witnessed arriving into the world at birth.

Baruti, Kimberley & little Baruti

"Education is an important element in the struggle for human rights. It is the means to help our children and people rediscover their identity and thereby increase self-respect. Education is our passport to the future, for tomorrow belongs to the people who prepare for it today."

Minister El Hajj Malik El Shabazz
(Malcolm X)

TABLE OF CONTENTS

Preface. 9

Introduction. 11

1. Preparing Your Child for the First Day . . . 15

2. Educating Your Child at Home
   (Preparation for the Parent). 29

3. Study Skills and Test Taking Strategies . . 51

4. "What Did You Learn Today?" 66

5. Parent-Teacher-Child Partnership 69

6. That Ever So Powerful Peer Group 75

7. A Note on Sleeping and Sugar Intake . . . 78

Conclusion 79

PREFACE

"A Black Parent's Handbook to Educating Your Children" is written as a contribution to the Black Liberation Struggle. True, it is an educational guide, but it is much more than the traditional sense of the word "education".

I am a Black man and I wrote "A Black Parent's Handbook" for Black people. This is not because I'm a racist or anything of this nature. It is because in order for us to rise to the level that we once occupied, WE MUST LIFT OURSELVES and stop depending on others to do it for us. This book therefore, is a contribution to that upliftment.

In reference to what we call ourselves, Black people in America have been identified by many different titles, including: negroes, coloreds, niggers, Blacks and Afro/Americans. It is now becoming very popular to identify ourselves as African/Americans. However, for this book, I have elected to use Black because this covers every person of African heritage in the world and I didn't want to leave anyone out.

In reference to gender (sex), I use his/her and he/she interchangably because "A Black Parent's Handbook" is written for both male and female parents and children.

I deliberately used a print size which is slightly larger than the norm, because in the

African tradition, our elders (grand-parents) play a very important role in the education of our children, so I therefore elected to use a print size that would be less difficult on the eyes to read.

Lastly, "A Black Parent's Handbook" is not a typical "reading" book. It is a book that should be used as a guide and read regularly and continuously in pursuit of the academic excellence of "our" children. I therefore included blank pages at the end for notes and left room in the margins for notes as well.

INTRODUCTION

Why this book anyway? When I was an undergraduate student, I majored in marketing. One of the first principles I learned in marketing (or selling) a product was there must be a need for your product. If there was no need for your product, it simply wasn't going to sell. In many cases, the public may not be aware that a need for the product exists, so it is therefore up to the business person to show the public that there actually is a need and that the satisfaction of this need will benefit the purchaser. The successful business person will even be able to show the public that they can't afford NOT to have the particular product being sold.

This is my motivation for writing "A Black Parent's Handbook". The need is there; it has been there for quite some time, but too few of us have been able to identify that the need actually exists. Everyday, we send our children to school and expect the school to do "our" job. It is true that the purpose of our children going to school is to receive an "education" (whatever that is), but that doesn't relieve us of our responsibilities as parents. We have a role to play as well. In fact, it is my opinion that we the parents should be the primary educators of our children and the schools should be considered supplemental. Afterall, these are our children and we should want to be their primary molders and shapers.

We the parents have to start taking a much more active role in the mental growth and development of our children. Too many Black children are performing poorly in school and unfortunately, many of the reasons are in fact beyond our immediate control. However, there is a great deal we can accomplish right now and this is where I make an attempt to fill a need in the Black community.

Our children are in school for approximately 6 hours per day. We must be abreast of all that is going on in their classrooms while they are in them. I'll get more into this in a later section. For now, we must keep in mind that when the 6 hours are completed, our children don't turn off their brains until the next day (we shouldn't allow them to, anyway). We must continue the educational process when they arrive home and challenge them to greatness at all times. We shouldn't expect anything less than greatness from our children.

Many Black children admire our Black giants in the sports and entertainment fields such as Michael Jordan, Mike Tyson, Whitney Houston, Janet Jackson, Michael Jackson and M.C. Hammer. However, I find that many young people (and adults) tend to take for granted the fact that these athletes and performers put thousands of hours of practice into their work to become the superstars that they are. True, they are obviously born with some level of potential, but it is the hard work and sacrifice that ultimately allowed them to become superstars.

This is the same thing we have to instill in our children. We have to push and challenge them, to and beyond their limits in order for them to reach their fullest potential. If all they do is go to school for 6 hours, come home and play, watch television and do a half hour of studying, then we as parents are short-changing our children and actually stunting their mental growth and development by not giving them the opportunity to maximize their fullest potential!

Through my own observations and experiences, I have found that for a multitude of different reasons, many parents are unaware of exactly what their responsibilities as "educators" of their children actually are. Many parents think the school is where all of the learning takes place or some think they lack the ability or expertise to do an adequate job in the home. It is my hope and desire that this book will remove any lack of confidence parents may have in becoming satisfactory educators of "our" children at home.

What I have sought out to do in "A Black Parent's Handbook" is to offer a few suggestions on "educating" your child outside of the classroom. I do not profess to be an expert, nor do I claim that "A Black Parent's Handbook" is complete. I write these thoughts only because there is a need (as evidenced by the high percentages of poor performances of our children in the schools among other things) and because I am a Black man who is committed to my people and will do anything to see even the slightest degree of progress towards liberation. In the African cultural tradition, it is not about each person individually working solely for themselves; it is about all of us working together collectively for the benefit of us all.

The writing style I have chosen is direct and to the point. You don't need a doctorate degree in order to understand this book. It is written for the parent who wants/needs quick answers and doesn't want to rack his or her brain to find them.

If I have made any errors in judgement or have written anything that appears offensive, I only blame myself and beg your forgiveness.

1.   PREPARING YOUR CHILD FOR THE FIRST DAY

It is the end of the summer and our children will be shortly returning to school. No matter what grade they will be entering, it is up to the parents to get them mentally prepared and motivated for what lies ahead over the next ten months. In other words, we want to put them on track and get them in the right frame of mind.

Ideally, it is the responsibility of the parents to keep the children motivated and focused all year long, which includes the summer months. As I stated previously, we have to push them hard. However, as the long hot summer comes to a close, it will be time to formally instruct them on what we the parents expect of them in the coming school year. This is the preparational stage. It's like anything else you set out to do. If you want something done correctly, you must prepare for it first. For example, let's say that two applicants for the same job must pass the same exam in order to get the particular job. Both are given a study guide which basically outlines everything that will be covered in the exam. One applicant studies and the other doesn't. The chances are good that the one who prepared himself will be the one who passes the exam and ultimately gets the job. It is the same thing with our children.

We have no business sending them to school to embark on something of such importance without the proper preparation first! Following are suggestions for preparing your child for that first day.

A.   Purpose of Going to School

The first suggestion is to discuss with your child his purpose for being in school in the first place. There are probably as many opinions for being in school as there are people. They include, to get an education, to get a good job, to make a lot of money, to go to graduate school, to start a business, etc. My purpose for writing "A Black Parent's Handbook" is not to define why a child should go to school. I will leave that to the parent to decide. However, I will say that whatever you decide is the purpose of your child's education, that you put it in the context of the Black community and not simply the individual child per se. What I mean, as I stated previously, is that we as Black people must be working in unity for our own upliftment. Therefore, if for example, your child wants to become a lawyer when she is an adult; from an African (Black) perspective, this would mean that the child would become a lawyer to allow her to defend other Black people against the vicious racism and oppression that we face on a daily basis. The money will come automatically if she is doing an adequate job and therefore need not be the focus.

In contrast, from a Euro-American (white) perspective, the purpose of a person becoming a lawyer is often to make a lot of money for himself, which places the community consciousness as secondary. We as Black people can't afford to think in these terms. We have to think in terms of our entire community or race FIRST, just as our ancestors who came before us did in order to get us to the level that we presently occupy.

Another example would be the youngster who desires to become the owner of a business when he becomes an adult. From an African (Black) perspective, this would mean that the child will start a business IN THE BLACK COMMUNITY in order to provide a viable and needed service FOR THE BLACK COMMUNITY, which in turn will keep our money IN OUR OWN HANDS as opposed to spending it with someone else who doesn't have the good of our community at heart. Also, this will enable the owner to hire other Black people to work for the growth and development of the business which will create even more jobs as opposed to having to search for employment in the Euro-American (white) community only to be denied because of the color of his skin!

So again, in discussing the purpose of

your child's education, be sure that it is from an African (Black) perspective, which will benefit us all, both collectively and as individuals.

B.   Time Spent on Homework and Studying

My second suggestion is to discuss with your children the amount of time to be spent doing homework and studying. This is something that should be outlined in advance. It's the same thing with a job. The employer theoretically explains to the employees in advance what is expected of them and therefore, the employees come to work knowing exactly what they are expected to do.

I recommend that a MINIMUM of two hours be spent doing homework, studying and preparing for the next day, in a quiet or as close to a quiet room as possible, with the television and the radio turned off! Rules should be established, written down and visibly posted regarding areas such as study time, television time, play time, etc. The television should not be viewed as a privilege, but as a sort of treat after everything has been correctly completed. I will speak more on the television in a later section.

C.   Classroom Expectations

My third suggestion is that you discuss with your children what you expect of them in their classrooms. For example, you would discuss what you expect of them in the areas of grades, performances, behavior in and out of the building, etc. It seems that too many parents have less than high expectations of their children. We should expect nothing but the maximum from them. If we don't EXPECT them to perform well in school, chances are good that they won't perform well. However, if we expect highly of our children, there is more of a likelihood of success because hopefully our high expectations will translate into pushing and challenging our children, to and beyond their limits.

When talking about grades and performances, it is always best to set concrete, specific, attainable goals. I have found that goal setting is extremely beneficial when you are out to achieve something. This provides you with an actual target to shoot for. The problem however, is that many of us are not clear on how to go about setting goals. For example, setting goals that are TOO HIGH or TOO LOW serves little if any purpose at all except to show us that we went about setting our goals incorrectly.

Below is a method that I have been using for quite some time, which has proven successful for me. I would like to share it with you and with a little creativity, you could apply this method to just about any endeavor that you

19

undertake.

D.   Goal Setting

I recommend that you assist your children in setting their goals on the afternoon of the first day of school, after they have shared with you the subjects that they will be learning during the school year. What you should do is assist them in setting concrete, specific, attainable goals for each subject area according to their individual strengths and weaknesses.

When I use the phrase, concrete, specific, attainable goals, what I mean are goals that are set, unchangeable, to the point, and realistically achievable. To make your goal concrete, it must be clearly definable and written down so that you can see it. A specific goal would be one clearly identifiable goal for each individual subject. An attainable or realistic goal would be a goal that is not beyond your reach. For example, let's assume that over the course of four years, your child has been a consistent low "C" student in science. Then setting a realistic goal for your child would be to achieve a "B". This is because your child has never maintained a "B" average previously and setting an "A" as the goal may prove too frustrating and discouraging an endeavor at this particular time.

Goal setting should be thought of as a staircase. It is ideal to set your goals up in steps or one step at a time. As we begin to progress, then we can start to skip steps. But while we are just starting out in this new endeavor of goal setting, we should proceed one step at a time. It's just as when a baby learns to walk up and down the stairs. In the beginning, the baby will walk one step at a time, using every step. However, as the baby matures and gains more confidence with the steps, he may then start to experiment with skipping steps. In setting goals, let's first go a step at a time and as we get better, we can then experiment with skipping steps.

On the other hand, if the student, again, is a "C" student in science, the goal should never be a "C" or below. This would not pose a serious challenge to the child. All he would have to do is the same quality and quantity of work he has done in the past. Remember, our objective as Black people is to push and challenge the children, to and beyond their limits so that they will be of useful service to the building and development of the Black community.

Once the "B" grade is achieved, the child can then go on to set an "A" as the goal. Once the "A" is achieved, the child must continue to work hard to maintain the "A" average.

Before moving on, I want to point out that there are basically two types of goals; short-range and long-range goals. The goals that I have been discussing thus far would be considered short-range goals. These consists of grades on tests, homework assignments, classwork and the marking period. In this context, the long-range goal would be the child's final or year end grade. This is the final average that the child is striving for. Going back to our staircase analogy, each step is a short-range goal and the top of the staircase would be the long-range goal.

Other long-range goals would be graduating from grammar school with a certain average; graduating from Jr. and Sr. High School with a certain average or being accepted into one of the prestigious Black colleges. Following is a description and model in setting up your child's goals.

First, each and every goal should be written down. This makes them more difficult to change than if they were only set in our minds. There is also less of a chance of forgetting them. Afterwards, your child's goal sheet should be posted in a visible area where you and your child can continuously review to determine whether or not the child is on track. Once the marking period is over, the child can compare the actual grades with the goals that were set and determine whether or not any revisions or adjustments will need to be made. After each marking period, a new goal sheet should be prepared.

On a large sheet of construction paper, the word "GOALS" should be written on top with the child's name written next to it. For example:

BARUTI'S GOALS

Underneath, on the left hand side, you would write the heading, "Current Status". The current status answers the question, "Where am I now and how did I get here?" In other words, you and your child must first determine where it is that he currently stands academically. In this section, you would list each subject and write next to each one, his current grade averages. This is done because in order to know where you are headed or going, you must know where you came from first. For example, if you were to ask someone how to get to New York, the first thing that they are going to ask is, "Where are you coming from?" If you are in Ohio and they give you directions from New Jersey, it's going to be very difficult to follow their directions to New York. However, if they know that you are coming from Ohio, it would be easy for them to provide you with proper directions.

Also, in your current status section, you should write the reasons for the current grades. You would state how many hours are currently spent studying, watching television, organizing, etc. This will assist you in identifying what needs to be changed and what should be maintained.

The next step would be to list your goals. This is when you actually set your goals for the marking period. Setting your goals answers the question, "Where am I going?" Your goals are where you want to go or be. They are the target that you are aiming for. Underneath the current status section, write down the subheading: "GOALS". Under goals, list each subject with the grade (goal) that your child will be aiming for beside it.

The third area of your goal sheet will be the strategy that your child will use to achieve his goal. Understand that it is one thing to SET a goal, but it is quite another thing to actually PURSUE the goal. You need a plan of attack in order to achieve your goals. You need to be able to determine what it is that you will need to do to achieve your goals. Your strategy answers the question, "How am I going to get there?" This is your plan of attack. Therefore, if for example, your goal was to achieve an "A" in science, your strategy may be to study science for one hour per day, to do extra projects, etc. It's similar to a football team after each play. For those of you who are unfamiliar with football, after each play, the team goes into a huddle to plan their next play. It is extremely rare that a team will have a play without a huddle first. In this huddle, the team is formulating a strategy to achieve their goals i.e., scoring touchdowns and ultimately winning the game.

Beneath the goals section, write down the subheading: "Strategy" and write the strategies that you and your child have agreed to use to achieve the goals.

Closely related to the strategies used are the tactics. The tactics are the specifics or details of the strategy. For example, if the strategy was to study science for one hour per day, possible tactics would include, studying and learning the vocabulary words, answering the chapter questions and learning the first ten pages of the chapter. This section, you can either keep separate or you can add to the bottom of your goal sheet. Keep in mind, that the tactics will constantly change in accordance with the specific work that is to be done. You'll need specific tactics for each area of work that you have to complete. Therefore, it would be best to prepare separate tactics for each assignment and tape these over the previous day's tactics. On the following page is an outline of how you and your child's goal sheet should look when completed.

BARUTI'S GOALS

I. Current Status (Where am I now?)
   (How did I get here?)
   A. Math
      1. Currently a "B" student
      2. Reasons:
         a.
         b.
         c.

   B. Science
      1. Currently an "A" student
      2. Reasons:
         a.
         b.
         c.

II. Goals (Where am I going?)
   A. Math - "A"
   B. Science - "A"

III. Strategy (How am I going to get there?)
   A. Math:
      1. Study 45 minutes per day.
      2. No television until all work is completed.
      3. Discuss all classwork and homework with parents.

   B. Science:
      1. Study one hour per day.
      2. No television until all work is completed.

IV. Tactics
   A. Math:
      1. Study pages 25 - 30.
      2. Complete the practice problems in the chapter.
      3. Have parents quiz me on problems.

   B. Science:
      1. Study pages 16 - 23.
      2. Define vocabulary words at the end of chapter.
      3. Answer practice questions at end of chapter.

Setting and writing goals, including the current status, strategy and tactics will allow your child to know exactly what it is that she has to do to succeed. It is all laid out and posted on the wall to review on a daily basis. This in turn develops organizational skills which your children will desperately need throughout their entire academic and professional careers.

Goal setting is an important part of academic success. Parents and children should work together in setting, reviewing and evaluating goals.

E.   Tools of the Trade

Another area of preparation is supplying the children with their "tools".   Just as a carpenter wouldn't or couldn't perform his job without tools, our children can't perform their responsibilities without their "tools" either. They need an adequate supply of pens and pencils, rulers, erasers, book covers, a notebook, paper and dividers.

I find that one problem with many children is that they are not organized.   They need looseleaf notebooks with dividers so that they can organize their work.   I urge you to purchase for them, looseleaf as opposed to coil binding because they need to be able to take sheets out, but also to insert them back into their proper places while maintaining neatness.   For example, their teacher may need to collect their work and check it.   However, the child may need to study from this assignment once it is returned from the teacher.   With a looseleaf notebook, the child can insert the work neatly back into the notebook in its proper place and have the work readily available for studying.

The child should have all of these items for the first day of school.   Now let's move on to see what areas the parents should be prepared, in order to educate the child at home.

2. EDUCATING YOUR CHILD AT HOME (PREPARATION FOR THE PARENT)

First, I want to make it clear that "A Black Parent's Handbook" is in no way an attack on the public school systems. My contention is simply that the schools cannot do the job of educating our children by themselves. This doesn't mean that I am in agreement with everything that goes on in the schools, however. It's just that I don't believe in solely attacking or criticizing a problem. I don't believe that solely attacking and criticizing bring about the desired results. I do believe in offering solutions which will bring about change in an expeditious, meaningful way. It is outside of the scope of this particular book to offer solutions to the problems of the school systems. What I am providing, however, are immediate solutions that we can begin to implement at home, which if seriously utilized, will ultimately carry over from the home into the classroom.

A. Schoolwork

Our children are our most precious gifts from our creator. We owe it to them to take an active interest in their academic development. One way of doing this is to learn along with them, their schoolwork or curriculum. In other words, we will be in a better position to assist our children in their studies if we read their school books and gain a general understanding of what they are studying. If for whatever reason, the child is not grasping the subject matter in the classroom, we can extend the instruction at home. But first, we need preparation. We have to study their books so that we are in a position to assist them in their education.

I understand that this may be time consuming and that many of you have many other responsibilities. However, we owe it to our children to find and create time to devote to their academic development.

B.   Reading

Reading is one of the most fundamental things that we can teach our children. It should be encouraged in the home each and every day. Through reading, a whole new world is opened up to our children. Every aspect of life is contained in books. For example, if someone wanted to learn about the history of Ancient Kemet (Egypt), the best way to learn about it would be to actually go there with a knowledgeable historian. However, if this were not practical or possible, the best alternative would be to read about it. This holds true with practically everything imaginable. All one has to do is pick up a book and begin to read.

The problem is that too many of us look at reading as a chore. We need to get out of this kind of thinking and begin to look at reading as a means of acquiring knowledge in order to liberate ourselves and our people. Through reading, we can learn such subjects as business, economics, politics, history and culture, medical care, prenatal and postnatal care, social service, psychology and sociology just to name a few.

As I stated previously, parents must encourage their children to read on a daily basis. You must teach your children the importance of reading. One of the best ways of doing this is for them to actually see you actively and enthusiastically reading as frequently as possible. They need to see that you value the pages of BOOKS. It is not enough to tell your children to read and yet not be a reader yourself. If they perceive that their parents don't value books, they will more than likely follow the parent's lead. If the parent values television and radio over books and newspapers, the children will probably value television and radio over books and newspapers as well.

We as Black people have to get our priorities in order and realize that we are in the midst of a liberation struggle. Too much music and television (the wrong kind of music and television) are not the vehicles to free our minds from the negative garbage that has been injected into them. We must replace the garbage with what has thus far been deliberately kept away from us. Therefore, when I say that we must read and that we must encourage our children to read, I don't mean that we must indiscriminately read anything. Our reading should be extremely selective and functional to aid and assist us in standing up as a liberated AFRICAN people!

Remember, we as Black people must be working in unity for our own upliftment. This means that we must develop a COLLECTIVE CONSCIOUSNESS with our history and culture as the foundation. What follows is the type of reading material that should take priority in our DAILY READING ROUTINE.

C.   African/Black History and Culture

Although this chapter is entitled, "Educating Your Child at Home", what actually is taking place is that not only is the parent educating the child but she/he is educating her/himself as well. It's simple common sense that in order to teach anyone anything, you must first acquire the knowledge that is relevant to what is to be taught. At this point, it will be appropriate to give a brief biographical sketch of myself to illustrate my contention.

Prior to 1984, I was a young Black man

who was basically just looking to get what I could out of life. I was a college student, but with no real sense of direction. My main activity was hanging out in the student center and interacting with friends. Since I didn't take my education seriously, I was virtually flunking out of school. I was a marketing major, but had no idea of what marketing was all about. If someone were to ask me what marketing was, I wouldn't have been able to explain it to them.

In terms of my Black consciousness level, I had none at all. If anyone said anything to me dealing with racism, apartheid in South Africa, Blacks in politics, Blacks in history or anything dealing with Black issues outside of sports and entertainment, my typical responses were, "I don't want to hear that sh-t" or "What's all that Black stuff gonna do for me?" or "that stuff's in the past; I'm dealing with the present" and other comparable ignorant statements like these.

The following year, I decided to enroll in another school as a last ditch effort to do well and graduate. Upon enrolling, I didn't really feel confident that I would succeed, but I was willing to give it one last try. I was 23 at the time.

During my second week of school, for some strange reason, I journeyed to the college library and sort of aimlessly roamed the aisles.

Unintentionally, I found my way to the Black studies section and noticed a book that was partially sticking out. I took it off the shelf and read the title: "To Kill a Black Man", by Louis Lomax. It was a book about the lives of Minister El Hajj Malik El Shabazz (Malcolm X) and Dr. Martin Luther King Jr. At the time, I knew very little about Dr. King and even less about Brother Malcolm. However, something compelled me to want to read this book. I therefore read it, but focused more so on the chapters dealing with Brother Malcolm. Something about this MAN intrigued and inspired me. Now I wanted to learn all I could about Brother Malcolm. I subsequently told a friend about the experience that I had in the library and the discovery of the book. He told me that he had read, "The Autobiography of Malcolm X", by Alex Haley in a Black studies course in college and that I could borrow the book.

Well my readers, I must say that this book completely changed and transformed my life. Brother Malcolm's life inspired me to want to achieve greatness. It was a sort of a rite of passage into manhood for me. Brother Malcolm's life inspired me to read everything that I could on Black people. I became a regular customer in many of the popular Black book stores in the New York/New Jersey area. I spent countless hours studying African history, culture and civilizations, African-American history, Caribbean history and anything that I could literally get my hands on dealing with the Black experience. I did all this reading while surprisingly maintaining a straight "A" average in college. Nothing could stop me at that point.

I finally graduated two years later with high honors, received numerous academic achievement awards and graduated as the top Black male student in my graduating class.

Again, it was my studying of Brother Malcolm that led me to study African history. This history served as a mirror for me and showed me who I am and who we are as an African people. When I came into the knowledge of the magnificence and greatness of our ancestors, I knew that I could achieve anything that I set out to achieve. School, in turn, became a breeze for me. I now knew who I was in history and understood that since our ancestors could accomplish the most complex endeavors, even under some of the most adverse circumstances, I could at least become an "A" student and graduate from college. Therefore, I proudly admit that it was reading Brother Malcolm's autobiography that transformed me from a boy to a proud, strong and committed Black Man!

The reason for such a transformation and radical change in my thinking was because through reading all of this relevant history, I was exposing myself to information about Black people that I never heard or read before. I had always heard derogatory, distorted and degrading accounts of Africa, but I had never heard anything positive or inspiring about it or in other words, the truth. Through studying Brother Malcolm, I learned that a large part of what opened his eyes was learning the truth about the history of Black people. Therefore, I was hungry for this same truth.

To give you a brief sketch of what I learned when I began to read; I learned that not only did man originate in Africa over 1.7 million years ago,[1] but that the Egyptian civilizations were African (Black) as well.[2] I learned that the Africans were in no way savage, as I was previously taught, but that our African ancestors were a highly civilized people. I learned about people like Imhotep, who was the world's first multi-genius. Not only did he design the first pyramid, which is called the Step Pyramid, back around 2980 B.C., but he was also the world's first physician, a wise man, a scribe, a chief lector priest, an astronomer, a magician, a poet, a philosopher and a healer. [3]

Two individuals who really fascinated me were two of the greatest military strategists that the world has ever produced: Hannibal and Shaka. [4]

Of profound significance to our history and culture was the strength of the African woman. I learned of many mighty African queens and leaders, such as Queen Hatshepsut, Queen Nefertiti, Queen Makeda (Queen of Sheba), Queen Candace, Queen Cleopatra, Nzinga and Yaa Asantewa.[5]

One era of our history that I found very intriguing was the era of the three magnificent empires of West Africa called Ghana, Mali and Songhay. These empires flourished from the 3rd century through the 17th century. Timbuctu, at that time was the greatest city in the world and the intellectual capital of these empires. It was the home of a university called the University of Sankore. This university attracted youth who wanted to study law and surgery from all over the Islamic world.[6]

In addition, during the same period, starting in the 8th century, an African people called the Moors went into Spain and occupied that land for 800 years and in the process, established a whole new, much more advanced way of life than what currently existed.[7]

When I began studying Blacks in America, I found out that Christopher Columbus didn't "discover" America at all, but that Blacks were in the Western Hemisphere building civilizations as far back as 800 B.C. [8]

There was one book that had a very profound impact on me and that book was entitled, "Black Inventors of America". In this book, I found that Black people, through their scientific genius, shaped the course of American industry despite being subjected to the most brutal oppression that the world has ever known. In this book, I learned that from the 19th century - 20th century, the Black man invented such inventions as the automatic transmission of the automobile, the refrigerated truck and boxcar, the electric railway system (subway), the rail car coupler system, the automatic lubrication system of a machine or engine, the traffic light, the gas mask, the shoe lasting (manufacturing) machine, the lawn mower and literally hundreds of other inventions right here in America.[9]

Of profound significance in relationship to inventors is the work of Lewis Latimer. I learned that this Black inventor deserves just as much credit for the invention of the light bulb as does Thomas Edison. This is because Edison's light bulb was highly impractical and continuously burnt out. Lewis Latimer invented the cotton thread filament which enabled the bulb to sustain its glow and was inexpensive to purchase. Latimer also drew the plans for Alexander Graham Bell's telephone patent. [10]

It is not surprising that Black Americans

have excelled in science and inventions when one considers the contributions that our African ancestors gave to the world, including science and technology, astronomy and astrology, architecture and engineering, education, mathematics, including algebra, geometry, trigonometry and calculus. They also gave us medicine, the first calendar, religion, philosophy, morals and ethics.

I cite these few contributions of Black people because our children need to know this. Our history is in fact, US! In the African tradition, we don't look at our history as being something detached from us. This history IS US. It is evidence of what we have done in the past and serves as a model and an example of what we can do in the present and in the future. It's just that we have to learn our true history, learn to appreciate it and carry it with us in our hearts and minds at all times.

I find that in many of the people who begin to learn and study the history of the Africans, start to make positive changes in their lives, drop negative habits, negative thinking and stand up to rise to the greatness of our ancestors. Many have argued that this is the reason that African history has been denied from our children for so long!

If the school system is unable or unwilling to teach our children the totality of their African history, then the burden lies on us the parents. We must become readers of everything that we can get our hands on relating to the history of the Black man and woman. However, in obtaining your books, you must be careful of who the authors are. In the majority of cases, I would recommend that you purchase books written by reputable and committed Black authors who see our history from our (African) perspective. In other words, if a Euro-American (white) person writes our history, in most cases, he is writing from his perspective or interpreting our history through a Euro-centric frame of reference. This therefore leads to an erroneous interpretation of our history. Only WE can accurately write and interpret OUR history. It's the same thing when you go to a library or bookstore and see books on European or white American history. It'll be a mighty cold day indeed, before you find many European or white American history books written by Black authors!

This is not to condemn Euro-Americans; it's just that in this day and age, we need our history interpreted from our own perspective.

You'll find that today, many of our children are not reading at grade level and are dropping out of school before graduation. I attribute a lot of this to the lack of a culturally relevant curriculum and culturally relevant reading material in many of the schools. In other words, the children are bombarded with images of non-Black people and therefore can't and don't relate to what they are reading and learning. As a result, they do not develop their reading skills, rapidly lose interest in school and ultimately drop out. It is up to the parent to counteract this absence of culturally relevant reading material by purchasing from Black bookstores as many books as possible about African/Black history and culture. You must set aside time to read these books in order to educate yourselves and your children.

It is also ideal to read to your children. Elementary age children love being read to and there is nothing wrong with this. By developing your interest and knowledge in African/Black history, you and your children will gain a new insight on life and will be inspired to accomplish greatness in the tradition of our African ancestors.

Another good idea is to form study groups in your community, to enable you to study and exchange ideas with other members of your community during designated times each week. This would be ideal for both the parents and the children.

There are many Black owned bookstores in the various different cities across the country and these are the stores that carry the books that you will need. I suggest that you don't waste your time looking in mainstream bookstores. The information on African/Black history and studies is scarce there and a lot of it is not written by Black scholars. I suggest that you therefore ask around for a good Black owned bookstore in your community if you don't know of any. In the conclusion, you'll find a suggested reading list to get you started on your quest for self knowledge.

Parents should also expose their children to African cultural events, such as lectures, speeches, documentaries, celebrations, plays, movies, and festivals. They need to be in environments where other Black people are expressing pride and joy in their history, culture and Blackness. In particular, they should go to events such as Kwanzaa festivities, Black History Month programs and take part in marches for justice.

Most importantly, I can't stress enough that your sons should have maximum exposure to our "Black Shining Prince", Malcolm X, who exemplifies manhood. Your daughters should have maximum exposure to Harriet Tubman, who exemplifies womanhood. I can't emphasize enough what the influence of Brother Malcolm's life did for my personal growth and development into manhood, which includes being a husband, a father and an educator.

D.   Black Media (Current Events)

Parents also need to expose their children to Black media. "Main stream" or white media gives the impression that Black people either don't exist or are basically criminals, rapists, drug dealers, murderers, prostitutes and corrupt politicians. This, incidentally also contributes to the low self-esteem that you find in many Black children. Reading Black newspapers will provide you with a much more accurate description of who WE are and what WE are all about. In addition, these papers provide us with a description of the problems that WE are afflicted with.

We need to buy Black owned newspapers and share them with our children. When the children are having current events, these are the papers that they should use for their particular articles. In this way, when for example a student brings in an article out of the white press that identifies the defendants in the New York City Central Park rape case as a "wolfpack", she can counteract this article with an article from the Black press that describes how the defendants weren't even in the park or how the DNA test proved that the defendants were the wrong people.

Above everything, let your children see you read SOMETHING! It is one thing to tell your children the importance of reading, but it is quite another thing for them to actually see you enthusiastically gaining new information and insight from the printed page. In other words, give them something of profound substance to emulate.

E.   Television

It is imperative that you the parent predetermine what your children are going to watch on television. I find that naive people view television as solely entertainment and informational. I reject this notion. There is a great deal of poison on television that is destroying the minds of Black people, children and adults alike.

Many of the shows on television that have Black actors and actresses usually cast these people in negative, stereotypical roles. They are usually comedies and Black people are usually the butt of all of the jokes. Visual images unfortunately, have much more of a lasting effect than do words. This is why a good teacher or a good salesman will use many visuals in a presentation. In television, these negative images are long lasting and damaging to our psyche. I would recommend that any show with Black actors and actresses that depicts Blacks negatively and stereotypically, you not allow your children to watch. If there were a counterbalance of shows depicting Black people as educators, lawyers, doctors, scientists, government officials, entrepreneurs, corporate vice presidents, etc., it wouldn't be as damaging. However, the majority of the shows, as I've stated, do Black people a grave injustice.

If your children are going to watch television, you the parent must determine in advance, what shows are psychologically healthy and what the maximum number of hours per day the children should be permitted to watch television. It should be kept at a minimum. Their time should be primarily devoted to educational-learning activities. However, if there is a good documentary or something comparable about the history, culture and struggles of Black people, it would be good to gather the family together to watch and to discuss the documentary at its conclusion to determine whether or not it dealt accurately with the topic.

F.   College/Career

No matter what grade or age of your child, he is never too young or too old to start thinking about college and a career. It would be ideal to begin to mention to him what college is and what a career is as soon as he is able to talk. Just hearing the words being spoken are planting seeds in his mind that you can cultivate as he gets older.

Nowadays, you find that a lot of people

are down on college because there are so many people who have spent 4+ years in college and have spent thousands of dollars on their education just to come out and not get hired for employment. However, this is because we have the wrong idea of why we should be attending college. During the enslavement of our ancestors, our purpose in life was to serve the master. "Physical slavery" is long over now, but we have yet to break the chains of "mental slavery".

What I mean is that if your child goes through elementary school for 8 years, high school for 4 years and then college for another 4+ years, shouldn't she now be equipped to do for herself? It seems to me that with all of the education that she has accumulated, she should now be able to apply it to the upliftment of herself and our people. For example, if your child were a business major, after 4+ years of college, she should be ready to start some type of small business (even if it's out of the home) to generate income for herself and to serve and benefit the Black community. This is just plain common sense. There is no need to envy someone else's accomplishments when we have the God given ability to do whatever it is that we desire. All it takes is an idea. Once the idea is firmly implanted into the mind, the next step is to convert it into reality!

When discussing a college education with your child, I strongly encourage you to interest your child in pursuing an education with a Black college. These colleges are just as good as any Euro-American (white) college and provide our young people with the type of environment that they will need to ultimately graduate and survive in a racist society.

You should also expose your child to many different careers. I find that many of our children who are on the streets doing nothing don't have a clue to the possibilities that are available to them. They hear of the traditional careers such as doctor and lawyer, but there are literally thousands of other possible options that they have simply never heard of or been exposed to. I would suggest that parents go to a local high school guidance counselor and ask for a book on careers. You could also go to a library or a local book store to find books and magazines dealing with careers and share these with your children. They need to know that despite the fact that racism is alive and kicking, they have the ability to overcome it if they are only aware of the possibilities that exist.

Other options are the trade and vocational schools for our children who are mechanically inclined. We as Black people not only need thinkers for our liberation, we need BUILDERS as well. Black people own very little in the Black community and therefore need to own and build our own structures for our own economic self-sufficiency.

Going back to the discussion on goals; college and career would be long-range goals. These, as all of the other goals should be written and visibly posted. In this way, your child will see the words "college" and "career" everyday of his life. Again, when you think of goals, think of them as a staircase with your short-range goals being the bottom stairs leading to the top of the staircase, which would be college and career, i.e. the long-range goals.

G.   Courses in Teaching

Another good preparational devise would be for you to enroll in a college or community college and take a few courses in teaching children; especially teaching reading. This can provide you with the theory and application of teaching your child. You may better be able to detect weaknesses and to diagnose these weaknesses. This will in effect assist you in conferring with your child's teacher about any problems which may occur.

H.   Board Games

It seems that board games do not have the same popularity that they once had, but board games can simultaneously be entertaining and educational. Board games have the ability to facilitate the mental growth and development of children if used correctly. I suggest that in the place of television, that certain evenings be designated as "game night". This would be the evening when the family comes together and plays a constructive board game. Games such as the word construction games or the Black History games encourage children to think and therefore you have your children in a situation where they are "working", but playing, enjoying work and learning at the same time. This also gives the family an opportunity to come together as one unit as opposed to everybody doing their own thing independently.

Another thought about board games is that although each person is competing against one another, parents should praise the children when they get a correct answer or move correctly, to reinforce positive responses. In other words, make them feel especially proud about doing things correctly and using their brains. This will stimulate them to perpetuate positive performance.

You can also get games that call for playing in teams. This provides for the opportunity to solve problems together as opposed to working individually. I feel that it is imperative that Black children learn to work TOGETHER, as opposed to against one another.

These eight areas: schoolwork, reading,

history-culture, Black media, television, college/careers, courses in teaching and board games are areas in which you can enrich yourselves in order to further educate your children outside of the classroom. This is not meant by any means to be all-inclusive or complete. These are just a few suggestions of how your time at home could be better spent with your children whom as I stated previously, are quickly and steadily losing interest in school, which the drop-out statistics will confirm!

3.   STUDY SKILLS AND TEST TAKING
      STRATEGIES

This is a chapter which actually could have been included in the preceding chapter, but I decided, after giving it careful thought and consideration, that it is a subject that deserves special attention.

Unfortunately, our school systems place a great deal of emphasis and importance on test results.   In most cases, test results are the primary means by which a student is evaluated. Many children may thoroughly understand whatever it is that they are learning, but for various different reasons, score poorly on the test.   For instance, some children panic at the sight of a test; some don't completely understand the wording of the test or are reading the questions too quickly or some are simply not good test takers.   In addition to these, there are some children who lack the skills or assistance from others in STUDYING for a test.

What we must keep in mind is that since the evaluation of our children is primarily based upon test scores, we must do all that we can to provide our children with the confidence they need in order to succeed at test taking. However, it is important that we don't send our children the wrong message, meaning that the purpose of their going to school is to score high on tests and to achieve high grades.   We want them to fully understand that they are there to learn! In other words, LEARNING COMES FIRST. As they become proficient in what they are learning, the grades will follow. But the emphasis should not be on grades first. This only leads to "beating the system", such as cheating or other methods of attaining high grades without actually learning what is being taught. Subsequently, it is up to the parent to assist the child in taking this knowledge and applying it to the unification, upliftment and building up of the Black community as I stated in chapter one. Following are suggestions on study skills and test taking strategies.

A.   Study Skills

Many children are told by their teachers and parents that they must study and do their homework regularly. However, the problem is that too many children lack good study skills and good study habits! Studying isn't simply going home and picking up a book and reading. In fact, that's more so what reading is, than studying. We don't want our children to simply go home and start reading; we want them to study as well.

To study, the children need to be in a room that is absolutely quiet, with no distractions. It would be ideal if they have their own desks as well. They also need a work area that is organized, tidy and well lit. In other words, they need to study in an ACADEMIC ENVIRONMENT for maximum results. Once they are organized and situated, they are then ready to study. Following are suggestions on how to study some of the subjects that your children may be learning. For those subjects that I have not listed, it is up to the parent to consult with the teacher or other qualified individuals to determine good study skills and habits for those particular subjects.

Your child's work area should be organized, tidy and well lit.

Spelling

First, the parent should check to ensure that all of the words on the child's spelling list are spelled correctly. There's nothing worse than learning to spell a word that is incorrectly spelled. Second, have the child write each word out, a MINIMUM of five times each, ONE WORD AT A TIME. I emphasize one word at a time because many children like taking the short cut and writing the words one letter at a time, underneath one another. It will be much more difficult to learn the proper spelling using this format however, because the emphasis is on speed.

In most cases, the teacher will give the class one week to learn anywhere from fifteen to twenty-five new words. Instead of attempting to learn all of the words in one study session or night, I strongly recommend that the list be broken down into segments, such as studying the first six or seven words on the first night, the second six or seven words on the second night and the last six or seven on the third night. In addition to this, you would review the words studied on the previous night, with the new words. On the fourth night, your child would start the cycle over, putting an emphasis on the first set of words again, but reviewing the others as well. This way, your child is keeping the words in the front of him and keeping them fresh in his mind. Also, by breaking the words down into groups or segments, your child isn't overwhelming himself with an entire list of fifteen to twenty-five words in one night.

After the words are written five times each, the child should say the words to himself and then write them without looking at the list. Afterwards, the parent or a partner should quiz the child on the first group of words to determine whether or not he has learned them and if not, to determine where the weaknesses are. This will enable the child to begin to build his confidence for the upcoming test. It is important however, that you do not let your child quiz himself, solely. He will need someone actually calling out the words just as it is done in the classroom. This, I feel is the best preparation. You would then continue this process all the way up to test time.

Vocabulary

For vocabulary words, as in spelling, the children are usually given a week to learn the definitions of approximately ten new words. Preparation for this test should also start on the first night.

When working with our children on their vocabulary words, we should frequently remind them of the importance that such great Black leaders as the Honorable Marcus Mosiah Garvey, Minister El Hajj Malik El Shabazz

(Malcolm X), Dr. Martin Luther King, Jr. and Rev. Jessie Jackson placed on learning new words in their youth and early adulthood. Each of these men at young ages wanted to expand their vocabularies. They understood the importance, value and power in having a repertoire of words. It is the wide range and usage of words that made these men in part, the great speakers that they were and still is in Rev. Jackson's case.

That is the context in which our children should learn their vocabulary. Teach them that it is the intelligent man or woman who knows many words and the many different ways to use words.

When studying their new vocabulary words, I suggest that the words be broken up into groups, just as the spelling words were. For example, if there are ten new words, I would suggest working on four to five at a time, in the same manner as the spelling words.

The first step would be to define the words. Now beware that just because a word is defined doesn't mean that the definition is clear. I strongly suggest that parents purchase for their children a good thesaurus (book of synonyms - words that have the same meaning) to determine exactly what these words mean and how they would be used in a sentence. Therefore, it would be good to purchase a thesaurus which contains example sentences as well. This will provide your child with a far superior understanding of what the words mean and how they are used.

I also suggest that you encourage your children to try to use these words in their everyday speech. It is when these words are actually used that they will really understand their meanings and feel comfortable using them.

Secondly, continue to define and put into sentences the words for each day, remembering to review the previous day's words as well. This way, by the end of the week, when it's test time, the child will have learned ten new words and in turn, will be prepared to score well on the test.

Once all of the words have been defined and are understood, you should quiz your children. You say the words and have him write the definitions and sentences. Another way would be for you to say the definitions and for him to write the words. Whichever way you decide is okay. Just remember that there is no reason why the child shouldn't be prepared at test taking time.

Math

With studying and understanding math, the key word is practice. First, it is imperative that the child pay attention to the methods of solving math problems in class. Second, she must, in addition to doing the homework problems, practice on as many similar problems as possible. The parent or someone else can make up problems and the child can be quizzed on them to determine whether or not she has mastered the skill.

There are also books and math dittos that can be purchased in bookstores, teacher supply stores and in some of the children's and toy stores. But the key thing is to have your child get as much practice as possible.

It is important that parents make the math as real and concrete as possible. In other words, the reason that many children have difficulty with math is because it appears to be abstract and not applicable to their everyday world. Therefore, the parent must show them why, for example, in developing the Black community, that numbers and calculations are an absolute necessity! They need to see the importance of numbers and math in terms of money, quantity of items, hours, dimensions in building new structures, etc. Whatever their field of interest, which they will hopefully use to contribute to the development of the Black community, the parent must be able to show the children how mastery of mathematics will apply. This is making the math meaningful and relevant to who they are as a Black (African) people.

In addition, it is ideal for the children to know how math relates to them from a historical perspective. For example, our African ancestors required proficiency in mathematics to construct the many pyramids, temples, obelisks and other massive structures in Ancient Kemet (Egypt), Nubia and Ethiopia. Without this knowledge of math, these structures wouldn't be what they are today. In fact, I would even venture to say that without exact calculations, these structures may not have survived the thousands of years that they have existed.

Science

Science is usually the subject that Black children have the most difficulty with and the least exposure to. There is a long history as to the explanation for this difficulty, which would require a whole different book, but I will say that we as parents must encourage our children to excel in science. Science is where the actual building up of our communities comes into play. We need Black engineers who can show us how to build new physical structures, such as buildings and factories in our communities. We need Black doctors to treat our sick at affordable prices with the care and attention that is required. We also need Black doctors to come up with new cures for the various sicknesses and diseases that plague the Black community.

We need more Black biologists, chemists and physicists. This is the context in which we should teach and work with our children when they study science.

Historically, science played a key role in African civilizations as well. Our children need to know that Africa produced the FIRST scientists, doctors and hospitals. They need to know that Africans were performing surgery and knew all parts of the body thousands of years ago. In other words, our children have to come to realize that by mastering these subjects, they are simply preserving and continuing the great legacy of our African ancestors.

As with all of the subjects, the studying of science should be an ongoing process. In most cases, the child will be provided with a text book and sometimes a work book. Most of his tests will come out of these two books. Therefore, the studying of these books should be on a regular basis.

I would suggest that the child learn the vocabulary words at the end of each chapter in the same manner as his weekly vocabulary words. However, he will not need a dictionary or thesaurus for these. The definitions are usually in the glossary contained in the back of the book. He should write the definitions and then see how the words are used in the paragraphs in the chapter to further understand the meaning and usage of the words.

In terms of studying the chapter, I would suggest that you and your child determine an amount of pages to be studied each day. It is important that your child read the sections more than once. In order to really learn, understand and memorize or retain information, it is important for that information to be repeated. It's similar to when you and your children listen to a song on the radio. The first time that you here it, chances are good that you won't be able to memorize the entire song, but as you hear it over and over, you begin to learn the lyrics even when you have no intention of learning them. Therefore, encourage your children to read the section of the chapter they are studying at least three times in order for it to stick. The three readings can be on the same day or preferably, on successive days. That is entirely dependent on your child's circumstances and timeframe, however.

I would also suggest that they write down in their notebooks, points that seem important and points that were learned in class. These are the areas that will more than likely show up on a test.

Always have your child answer the questions at the end of the chapter if they are not already assigned for homework. This will provide him with further practice in his studying.

Lastly, don't forget to quiz your children on the work that they have studied. Remember, send them to school prepared to excel, not to fail!

In terms of studying for social studies, the same study techniques basically apply, so I will not go further into this.

These are just a few helpful suggestions. Obviously, there are other subjects that your children are studying, but hopefully these suggestions will give you some ideas on what you have to do to assist your child with his studying in other areas.

B.   Test Taking Strategies

As I stated at the outset, for various different reasons, many of our children have mastered the subject material, get to the test, PANIC and fail. Another cause of failure is that the questions are misread because the child didn't take her time reading them. Lastly, the problem may be that the child is simply not a good test taker. Following are suggestions for overcoming these short-comings.

Panic

If you and your child worked hard together in preparing your child for the test, there is absolutely no need for panic, especially if she has been previously quizzed, shown her mistakes and has strengthened her weaknesses. Relax your child by reassuring her that she has worked hard, prepared herself and has mastered the subject material.

Also be sure that your child gets a good nights rest and has a good hot breakfast. Remember in the morning to ease your child's anxieties by reminding her that she is thoroughly prepared for the test.

Misreading Questions

Encourage your child to take her time, but not to work too slowly when taking the test. Remind her that she is prepared, to carefully read the questions and to think and concentrate while taking the test. Above all, remind her to read the entire question carefully.

Things to Look for in Test Questions

In taking a test, it is important that a child know how to read a test question and know what to look for in reading the question. For example, in a true/false test, be careful of the words: "always" and "never". If a test question in a true/false test read, "Birds ALWAYS fly south"; if the child is not thinking, he may select "true", because he is associating birds with flying south when the weather gets cold in the north.

However, this does not mean that they ALWAYS fly south. This means that SOME birds fly south DURING THIS PARTICULAR TIME OF THE YEAR. But again, the question states that "Birds ALWAYS fly south". The answer to this question would therefore be false.

In multiple choice tests, again, have your children prepared for "always" and "never" and other absolute or all inclusive words or phrases. Also, when taking a multiple choice test which has three or more possible answers, first teach your child to eliminate the choices that he clearly knows are incorrect and to work with the remaining answers. There's no sense in working with the choices the child knows are incorrect.

If your child is taking a test using a fill-in-the-blank format, remind him to read the entire sentence before answering the question. Sometimes, the answers can be identified within the context of the sentence. For example, in the sentence, "Malcolm X made the_____ to Mecca and saw thousands of other pilgrims", reading the entire sentence gives you clues. However, if the child stopped at the word "Mecca", he is not getting all of the clues. By reading the entire sentence, he reads the most important context clue, "pilgrims" and now has a better chance of coming up with the correct answer, "pilgrimmage".

Encourage your children to spend

minimal time on questions that they do not understand and to work on the questions that they do know the answers to. Teach them to come back to the questions that they are having difficulty with, after they have completed the easier questions.

There are several other types of tests that a teacher may administer to the class, but I used these three because they are common and as examples, in order for you the parent to better identify what to look for in your child's particular circumstances.

Lastly, I wrote this chapter with the assumption that parents always know when the child is having a test. IT IS IMPERATIVE THAT PARENTS KNOW EVERYTHING THAT GOES ON IN THE CHILD'S CLASSROOM, INCLUDING KNOWING WELL IN ADVANCE WHEN THE CHILD WILL BE GIVEN A TEST. This way, the parents are in a better position to assist the child in his preparation for the next test.

4.   "WHAT DID YOU LEARN TODAY?"

"What did you learn today?" These five simple words are so important and yet, with many parents that I have spoken with, they are absent from their everyday speech. I dare say that the first thing you should say to your child when you see him in the evening is "What did you learn today?" (after saying hello, of course).

To put this into perspective, we send our children to school for approximately 6.5 hours per day. That comes out to 32.5 hours per week, 130 hours per month and 1300 hours per school year. Therefore for 1300 hours per year, our children are in the hands of someone who we probably know very little about, yet we expect this person to "educate" our children. Don't get me wrong. Most of the teachers in the various school districts are excellent, talented teachers and are strongly committed to our children's development. However, these are our children and we should be curious enough to at least want to know what they are learning in school.

By asking your child what he learned, you are giving him an opportunity to articulate what his day was like and how it was spent. This will in turn reinforce what was covered during the day and indicate to you if your child is having difficulty with the lessons.

Frequently, a child who is shy will not

raise her hand to volunteer information and eventually, the teacher finds her favorites in the students who volunteer. Consequently the teacher has no way of knowing whether or not the shy student is grasping the information. The exam will be the only indicator, but with reinforcement from verbal communication, the student may have been better prepared to take the exam.

Also in the classroom, you find that many teachers are still using the traditional methods of teaching, with the teacher doing practically all of the talking. By asking your child what he learned in school today, your words are actually minimal and the child will have the opportunity to do the talking. He should be comfortable because he is in his most familiar environment, i.e. home. If the child doesn't say much, you know that something is wrong and it is therefore up to you to get to the bottom of the problem.

You should have your child show you in his notebook what he did in class that particular day, including current homework assignments. If he has nothing to show you, it is up to you to find out why. He should also have his school books so that you can work together on whatever he is having difficulty with.

In my experiences that I have had in teaching, I have found that students will complete their homework, but in some cases the work will be drastically incorrect. This is an indication to me that the parents didn't inspect the work. In a lot of cases, the parents will instruct the children to do their homework, but they won't check the accuracy of their child's work. This is not fair to the child because he is not being challenged to the fullest. I understand that many parents are working more than one job just to make ends meet, but somehow, we must fit our children into our routine as well. If it is simply impossible, then it would be helpful to ask another family member (including extended family or friends) to lend assistance to ensure that the child is getting the attention that he deserves at home.

In addition to inquiring into your child's day, it would also be good to have set times when you simply talk and have conversations and discussions with your children. For example, instead of watching television at a particular time, time could be used to have a family conversation or discussion about almost anything. This way, you can gain further insight as to what is on your children's minds. These sessions would be good to discuss subjects such as AIDS, sex/pregnancy, racism, homelessness or anything else in academics, current events or social concerns.

5. PARENT-TEACHER-CHILD PARTNERSHIP

This chapter's focus is on the importance of teamwork. I have witnessed over the course of my life that a team of individuals working together in unity towards a single common goal is always more effective than a group of disunified individuals working separately trying to accomplish everything independently. A classic example would be the Detroit Pistons championship basketball team of '89 and '90. This is a team where arguably, not a single player stood out above the rest. Each player was working together as a single unit to accomplish one common goal; to win the NBA title. There was not one individual player on the team that appeared to be out for himself.

In contrast, many of the NBA teams of those two seasons did not measure up to the Detroit Pistons. This is in no way due to any lack of talent, but because they didn't have the same level of unity, cohesiveness and chemistry as the Detroit Pistons. On many teams, you find players who are only concerned about their own individual statistics. The end result is that these teams either suffer losing records or fair poorly in the playoffs against cohesive, team-oriented ball clubs.

My point is that in order to get a job done that involves two or more individuals, these individuals need to be coordinated in a kind of way that will allow them to work as a unified, common goal directed, team or unit.

What does this mean to you, the parents? It could possibly mean the educational success or failure of our children. In other words, when we think of the parents, the child and the teacher, we have to stop thinking of these people as distinct individuals and begin to think of them as a team or as one unit working TOGETHER for a common goal and purpose; the educational achievement of the child.

Parents are here to nurture their children. Teachers are here to teach the children. The children are here to learn so that they will be able to one day assume the role of productive adults. It therefore makes much more sense for these individuals to come together as a collective whole.

I find far too often that the parents dislike the teacher, the teacher dislikes the child, the child dislikes the teacher, etc.. This arrangement is not conducive to the academic success of the child. The child winds up being the one who suffers most from these antagonisms and hostilities!

The way to correct this situation is for all parties involved to grasp a full understanding of their roles. In other words, what are the roles of the parents in relationship to their children? What is the role of the teacher in relationship to the child? What is the child's role in relationship to both the parents and the teacher? And what is the role of the teacher and parent in relationship to one another? This must be fully resolved from the outset because too many parents are placing an excessive amount of the burden on the teachers; too many teachers are placing an excessive amount of the burden on the parents and the children are left unaware of the responsibilities that they should be assuming for themselves.

Since "A Black Parent's Handbook" is written to and for parents, as opposed to teachers, I will make my suggestions and recommendations to the parents.

It is imperative in these times of drop-out rates in epidemic proportions, that the parents make contact with the teacher as close to the first day of school as possible and arrange for an initial in person meeting. In this way, both the parents and teacher can gain an understanding of one another and learn what each expects of the child. The parents can learn from the teacher in what way they can be of assistance to the child in her schoolwork at home. The parents can also gain insight into the teacher's background, prior successes and failures, teaching style, level of committment, Black consciousness level, goals and vision of the future. In this way, you the parents are showing the teacher your level of committment to your child's academic achievement as well. Subsequently, these meetings should be arranged as often as needed. The parents should and have every right to get an update on their child as often as is necessary.

It is unfortunate that so many parents will go a full year without at least on one occasion, meeting the teacher of their children. As I stated previously, the child is with this teacher for approximately 1300 hours per year. We should at least desire to know SOMETHING about anybody spending this much time with our children.

Another problem is that the parents and teacher don't get to meet one another until there is a problem. I recommend that instead of waiting for a problem, that the parents set out to prevent the problem from occurring. When the child realizes that the parents and teacher are or will be in close contact with one another regarding his progress, the child will be more inclined to take his education much more seriously than he would if his parents showed no interest in his progress. By knowing that his parents frequently confer with his teacher, he knows that his parents are interested in his achievement.

Now we are in a situation where we have

a cohesive team or in other words, the parents are working with the child at home, the parents are interacting with the teacher and the teacher is working with the child in the classroom. ´It would be ideal if once or twice per marking period, in addition to the parent-teacher meeting, that the parents, teacher and child could have "progress conferences" where all have the opportunity of being present and everyone can gain a better understanding of their individual roles. This is what strengthens the team or collective orientation, which is vital.

Taking this time to discuss your child's progress with his teacher will give you an indication as to what measures you need to take at home. However, I find that there are many parents who would like to meet with their children's teachers, but because of such things as a large gap in educational levels or socio-economic status, some parents are hesitant or intimidated about meeting with the teachers. Consequently, the parents never take the opportunity to meet with the teacher and the end result is that the child is the loser.

In response to this, I say to the parent that there is no need whatsoever to be intimidated by your child's teacher. The teacher is there to educate your child and to confer with you as often as necessary. In most cases, the teacher is eager to meet with you because the teacher knows that if you are working with the child on your end, his job will be less difficult, especially in the area of discipline. This will provide the teacher with more time to teach.

Parent, child and teacher should work together as a partnership.

So again, meet with your child's teacher. Form a working partnership which in the long run will benefit everyone involved: child, parents and teacher.

6. THAT EVER SO POWERFUL PEER GROUP

The topic of the peer group is an area of special concern because the influence that the peer group exerts on its members can be overpowering! The peer group's influence is so strong that it has the potential to destroy all of the efforts that you have put into nurturing, educating, socializing, molding and shaping your child. It is therefore necessary that we pay particular attention to the peer group and its powerful influence.

Your child's peer group is generally his friends and associates. They are usually of the same age and socio-economic background. They usually develop similar attitudes, values, opinions and behavioral patterns. These characteristics can be good if they are positive, productive characteristics. The problem, however, is when the peer group exhibits negative characteristics.

Many children have a strong need to be accepted by their peers. In other words, they want to be "in" with the crowd. When they are not accepted by their peers, they have the potential of developing feelings of rejection which can lead to low self-esteem, self-doubt and low self-worth. This is devastating for a child and the end result could possibly sap his ability and motivation to maximize his capacity to become what he potentially has the ability to become.

On the other hand, if this group is engaged in negative behavior, exhibits a warped value system or engaged in behaviors that are not conducive to the upliftment of Black people, it will be difficult to control the influence that they have on your child if they are fulfilling your child's need to be accepted.

I would recommend first that you always teach your child positive values at home. This is in line with teaching your child African history and especially African culture, which includes an African value system. If the parent is not teaching positive values at home, the child is going to develop her value system either in the street, or through the media, such as television and movies.

Secondly, I would suggest that parents meet and get to know all of their child's friends (peer group). In this day and age, parents can't afford to allow their children to go outside, with parents not knowing who their children are spending their time with. It is important that parents know their children's friends. This way, they can determine whether or not their children should be friendly with these particular friends. For example, if the child's friends come from homes where positive values are not stressed and the friends are already starting to engage in negative behavior, the parents will be in a position to decide whether or not their child should maintain a relationship with these particular friends. If the parents don't know their children's friends, it will be difficult to determine what their friends are like solely from the description of the child.

I would also suggest that in addition to getting to know the friends of your children, that you get to know the parents of your children's friends as well. This way whether the friends have positive or negative values, you will be in a position to gain more insight as to why the friends have the values that they have, through their parents. As a result of meeting other parents, the parents could even form a sort of partnership to work together in the social development of the other children. In other words, now the children will know that not only will they have to answer to their own parents, but they will also have to answer to the parents of their friends as well. This is the way that things were done many years ago and this is in the African tradition.

7. A NOTE ON SLEEPING AND SUGAR INTAKE

We are all guilty sometimes, of taking our rest for granted. However, it is important that our children receive the proper rest before going to school in the morning. Elementary age children have no business staying up late at night watching television. They should be in bed by 9:00 p.m. and absolutely no later than 10:00 p.m.!

In order for them to be alert, attentive in class and ready to engage in their home after school educational activities, they need a good nights rest and a well balanced diet.

Lastly, I strongly recommend that you monitor your child's sugar intake, especially in the morning. I find that a lot of our children are overly hyper and excited throughout the course of a day and a lot of this is attributable to large amounts of sugar intake, including cereals, candy, juices, etc. Such a large amount of sugar is not good for your child's physical or mental growth and development. It would therefore be to you and your child's benefit to keep the sugar intake at a minimum.

CONCLUSION

I hope that my suggestions will be of some use and value to you and your children. As I stated in the introduction, I don't profess to be an expert or authority on the subject, but just a Brother who is serious about the upliftment and liberation of all Black people, wherever they may be.

You owe it to yourself and your children to at least give these suggestions an opportunity to work. Also, be creative and add your own ideas as they come to you. It would also be good to interact with other parents in order to exchange ideas on this topic. I say that whatever it takes to save our Black children, let's do it together.

Following is a list of books that I recommend you read to get you started on your search for the truth of who we are as an African people. The list is by no means all-inclusive or complete. It is only a starter list to get you going. Just about all of these books can be found in any Black bookstore.

PEACE

SUGGESTED READING

African History

1. Black Man of the Nile -
                    Dr. Yosef ben-Jochannan
2. Introduction to African Civilizations -
                    John G. Jackson
3. The African Origins of Civilization -
                    Dr. Cheik Anta Diop
4. Stolen Legacy -
                    George G.M. James
5. Destruction of Black Civilization -
                    Chancellor Williams
6. World's Great Men of Color, Vols I and II -
                    J.A. Rogers
7. Sex and Race, Vols I-III -
                    J.A. Rogers
8. Introduction to African Religions -
                    John Mbiti

African/American History

1. Before the Mayflower -
                    Lerone Bennett, Jr.
2. From Slavery to Freedom -
                    John Hope Franklin
3. Peculiar Institution -
                    Kenneth Stampp
4. Miseducation of the Negro -
                    Carter G. Woodson
5. Philosophy and Opinions of Marcus Garvey
                    Amy Jacques Garvey
6. Marcus Garvey, Hero -
                    Tony Martin
7. Marcus Garvey and the Vision of Africa -
                    Dr. John Henrik Clarke

8. Up From Slavery -
                              Booker T. Washington
9. Life and Times of Fredrick Douglass -
                              Frederick Douglass
10. Harriet Tubman -
                              Ann Petry
11. Autobiography of W.E.B. DuBois

12. Autobiography of Malcolm X

13. Malcolm X Speaks -
                              George Brietman
14. Malcolm X, The Man and the Times -
                              Dr. John Henrik Clarke
15. King, A Biography -
                              David Lewis

Education

1. All of Jawanza Kunjufu's books
2. Black Children - Janice Hale Benson
3. I Cry for my Parents - Mia Isaac

Psychology

1. Developmental Psychology of the Black Child
                              Amos Wilson

2. Chains and Images of Psychological Slavery
                              Dr. Naim Akbar

Miscellaneous Titles

1. Afrocentricity -
    Molefi Kete Asante
2. Black Men -
    Haki Madhubuti
3. Black Skin/White Mask -
    Franz Fanon
4. How Europe Underdeveloped Africa -
    Walter Rodney
5. They Came Before Columbus
    Ivan Van Sertima
6. Blacks in Science -
    Ivan Van Sertima
7. Black Inventors of America -
    McKinley Burt, Jr.
8. Introduction to Black Studies -
    Maulana Karenga
9. Kwanzaa -
    Maulana Karenga
10. The Choice -
    Sam Yette
11. The Souls of Black Folks -
    W.E.B. DuBois
12. Black Boy -
    Richard Wright
13. What They Never Told You in History
    Class-
    Kush

Children's Titles

Most of the children's books written by Black authors are
excellent. Read them first, however, before sharing them
with your children.

FOOTNOTES

Section Two

1. ben-Jochannan, Yosef. Black Man of the Nile and His Family. New York: Alkebulan Books Associates. 1970. pp. 94-95

2. Diop, Cheik Anta. The African Origins of Civilization: Myth or Reality. Westport: Lawrence Hill and Co. 1970. pp. 1-9

3. Rogers, J.A. World's Great Men of Color, Vol. I Introduction by Dr. John Henrik Clarke, New York: Macmillian Publishing Co. 1972. pp. 38-46

4. Ibid, pp. 98-109, 265-275

5. Diop, Cheik Anta. The Cultural Unity of Black Africa. Introduction by Dr. John Henrik Clarke. Afterword by James Spady. Chicago: Third World Press. 1978. pp. I-XV

6. Bennett, Jr., Lerone. Before the Mayflower: A History of Black America. Chicago: Johnson Publishing Co., Inc. 1982. pp. 13-22

7. Jackson, John G. Introduction to African Civilizations. Introduction by Dr. John Henrik Clarke. Secaucus: The Citadel Press. 1970. pp. 157-193

8. Van Sertima, Ivan. They Came Before Columbus. New York: Random House. 1976. pp. 142-174

9. Burt, Jr., McKenley. Black Inventors of America. Portland: National Book Company. 1969. pp. 136-143

10. Karenga, Maulana. Introduction to Black Studies. Los Angeles: Kawaida Publications. 1982. p. 121